EDGE
BOOKS
™

THE KIDS' GUIDE TO

PRANKS,

tricks,

and

PRACTICAL JOKES

by Sheri Bell-Rehwoldt

Capstone
press®

Mankato, Minnesota

Edge Books are published by Capstone Press,
151 Good Counsel Drive, P.O. Box 669, Mankato, Minnesota 56002.
www.capstonepress.com

Library of Congress Cataloging-in-Publication Data
Bell-Rehwoldt, Sheri.
    The kids' guide to pranks, tricks, and practical jokes / by Sheri Bell-Rehwoldt.
    p. cm. — (Edge books. Kids' guides)
    Includes bibliographical references and index.
    Summary: "Provides instructions for pulling a variety of harmless pranks,
tricks, and practical jokes" — Provided by publisher.
    ISBN-13: 978-1-4296-2275-2 (hardcover)
    ISBN-10: 1-4296-2275-X (hardcover)
    1. Tricks — Juvenile literature. [1. Jokes.] I. Title.
GV1548.B43 2009
793.8 — dc22   2008029689

Editorial Credits
Christopher L. Harbo, editor; Bobbi J. Wyss, designer;
    Marcy Morin, project production

Photo Credits
Capstone Press/Karon Dubke, cover, 1, 17 (bottom right), 21, 30; TJ Thoraldson
    Digital Photography, all other interior photos
Ed Shems, all spot illustrations

1 2 3 4 5 6 14 13 12 11 10 09

TABLE OF CONTENTS

You probably picked this book because you're a practical joker. Maybe you need a new prank to horrify your little sister. Or you're looking for an amazing trick that will blow the socks off everyone you know. You've come to the right place!

Of course, you don't want to get into any serious trouble. The tricks and pranks in this book won't hurt anyone. And they won't damage cars, houses, or pets. They might, however, really steam up your friends!

4

This book is just the beginning of all the fun you can have with pranks and tricks. When you've used these tricks, try to think of your own. But consider yourself warned. Start down this path and you can expect your victims to dish up some serious payback.

5

DRIPPY

This easy prank will leave your **victims** all wet. They'll never suspect a thing when you hand them what looks like a normal cup.

What You Need
* sewing needle
* plastic cup
* water

Step 1: Use a sewing needle to poke several holes in the middle of the cup. Store the cup in a safe place until a friend says she's "dying of thirst."

Step 2: When you hear those magic words, jump up and smile sweetly. Then offer to get her a cool drink.

Step 3: As you fill the cup, cover the holes with your thumb so the water doesn't pour out. Then hand over the cup with the holes facing your victim. She will think you're being nice – until she drinks from the cup and water dribbles down her shirt!

TIP: THE TIME TO SLINK AWAY IS WHEN SHE TIPS THE CUP.

6

Impressiveness: ★★☆   **Complexity:** ★☆☆

SAY CHEESE

What You Need

* sliced bread
* individual cheese slices wrapped in plastic

Nearly everyone likes a cheese sandwich. But no one will like this recipe!

Step 1: Offer to make your victim a cheese sandwich.

Step 2: Make the sandwich, but "forget" to remove the plastic wrapping on the cheese.

Step 3: Hand your victim the sandwich. Then get ready to apologize after he bites down on the plastic.

TIP: THIS PRANK WORKS BEST WITH VICTIMS ON WHOM YOU'VE NEVER PLAYED FOOD TRICKS.

Impressiveness: ★☆☆   Complexity: ★☆☆

LET 'ER RIP

What You Need
* cloth rag

If there's one practical joke that's perfect for a public place, this is it. Why? Because you want your victim surrounded by others when you let 'er rip!

Step 1: Rip the rag into long strips. Each strip should be about 2 inches (5 centimeters) wide.

Step 2: Start a new rip in each strip that is about 2 inches (5 centimeters) long.

Step 3: Hide the strips in your pocket until you're ready to pull the prank.

Step 4: "Accidentally" bump an item belonging to one of your friends onto the ground. Have one of your strips ready.

Step 5: When your friend bends down to pick it up, rip the strip in half.

RRRRIIPP

SALE!

Expect to hear lots of laughs as your victim reaches back to feel if his pants are ripped!

Impressiveness: ★★★   **Complexity:** ★★☆

BEACH BOMB

What You Need

* beach towels   * sandy beach   * sand shovel

Nothing's quite as fun as a day at the beach. And with this prank, the fun will double. That's because with just a bit of muscle power, your victim will sink to a new low!

Step 1: Lay your towel out on the beach, close to your friend's towel. Keep your sand shovel hidden.

Step 2: When your friend leaves for the snack shop, pull back his towel. Quickly dig a hole in the center. The deeper you dig the hole, the better. Cover the hole by spreading the towel back over it.

Step 3: Act completely surprised when your friend sinks into the hole when he returns. Blame the hole on sand crabs!

Impressiveness: ★★   **Complexity:** ★☆

SHAKE, RATTLE, AND ROLL

What You Need

* letter-size envelope
* marker
* wire coat hanger
* wire cutters
* rubber band
* large coat button

Do you have friends who are squeamish about snakes? This prank is perfect for them. But be warned, some of your pals might wet their pants. Don't stand too close!

Step 1: On the outside of the envelope, write "Rattlesnake Eggs. Handle with Care."

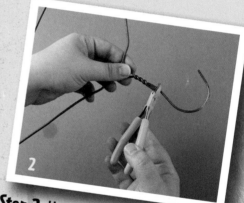

Step 2: Use wire cutters to snip the curved hook off of the coat hanger.

Step 3: Slip the rubber band through two holes of the button. Loop the ends of the rubber band over the ends of the U-shaped wire that you cut in step 2.

Impressiveness: ★★★   **Complexity:** ★★☆

Step 4: Wind the button until the rubber band is twisted tightly. Place the button inside the envelope. Grasp the button through the envelope with your other hand to keep it wound up.

RRAAAAATTLE

RATTLESNAKE EGGS

TIP: DON'T LET YOUR FRIENDS SEE INSIDE THE ENVELOPE BEFORE THE RATTLING BEGINS.

Step 5: Invite your friends to view the rattlesnake eggs you're babysitting until they hatch. When they gather around, open the envelope so they can peek inside. Then let go of the button and watch them jump. They'll think your noisy little snakes have hatched and are about to strike!

YOU SNOOZE, YOU LOSE

What You Need

* a bed with top and bottom sheets of the same color or pattern

One sneaky way to get back at brothers and sisters is to short-sheet their beds. You'll need about 5 minutes in their bedrooms, so wait until they're taking a shower!

Step 1: Carefully study how the bed looks before you touch it. You must make sure it looks exactly the same when you're finished.

Step 2: Remove the top sheet and any blankets. Leave the bottom sheet on the mattress.

Step 3: Spread the top sheet out over the bottom sheet. Then tuck the top sheet under the mattress at the head of the bed instead of the foot of the bed.

Step 4: Grab the loose edge of the top sheet at the foot of the bed. Fold it up toward the head of the bed. You've just created a U-shaped sack.

Step 5: Cover the sheet with the blankets, pillows, and other items that were on the bed before you started. Then split so you don't get caught. You'll know by the shouts that your prank was successful!

13

LAUGHING THROUGH THE TEARS

What You Need

- ★ wax paper
- ★ cookie sheet
- ★ nonstick cooking spray
- ★ 1 small apple
- ★ 3 apple-sized onions
- ★ 4 wooden caramel apple sticks
- ★ 1 14-ounce (400-gram) package of caramels, unwrapped
- ★ small cooking pot
- ★ 1 tablespoon (15 mL) water
- ★ spoon

This practical joke really brings on the tears because these caramel "apples" are made with onions!

Step 1: Lay a long piece of wax paper over a cookie sheet. Spray the paper with nonstick cooking spray.

Step 2: Wash and dry the apple. Then pull off the stem.

Step 3: Remove the papery outer layers of the onions.

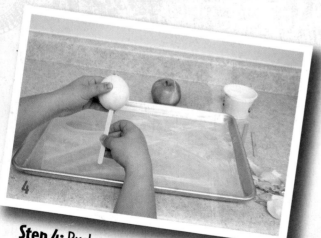

Step 4: Push a wooden stick into one end of each onion. Also push a stick into the stem hole of the apple.

Step 5: Dump the caramels into a small cooking pot. Add the water. Melt the candy over low heat, stirring it with a spoon until it's smooth.

Step 6: Dip the apple in the hot caramel sauce, covering it completely. Place it on the wax paper. This one is for you!

Step 7: Dip the onions in the hot caramel sauce until they also are completely covered. Place them on the wax paper, slightly away from your apple.

Step 8: Place the cookie sheet in the refrigerator for one hour to cool the caramel.

Step 9: Invite your friends over for a tasty treat. Set the cookie sheet on the counter 15 minutes before they arrive, so the caramel softens.

Step 10: Before handing out the onions, take a bite of your apple. Make sure your friends see that it really is an apple. When they chomp into their onions, you'll get a good laugh from seeing their sour faces!

Impressiveness: ★★☆   **Complexity:** ★★☆

PSST! HERE'S THE POOP!

What You Need

* ¼ cup (60 mL) creamy peanut butter
* microwavable bowl
* chocolate syrup
* spoon

If you have a kid brother who is potty training, this practical joke will get your mom hopping mad! Just be sure to **confess** your joke so your brother doesn't get in trouble. And don't pout if your mom makes you clean up the mess. It will be worth it!

Step 1: Put the peanut butter in a microwavable bowl.

Step 2: Squirt a little chocolate syrup in the bowl. Use the spoon to mix it into the peanut butter. Keep adding chocolate syrup until it becomes as dark as you want it to look.

Step 3: Put the bowl in the microwave and set the timer to 10 seconds on high. This should make the mixture thinner.

Step 4: Let the peanut butter cool for 1 minute.

Step 5: Wipe the "poop" across the seat of the toilet. Then act disgusted as you call your mom in to see the "gift" your little brother left behind!

16

« **confess** to admit that you have done something wrong »

Impressiveness: ★★★   **Complexity:** ★☆☆

GAG·O·BARF·O·RAMA

What You Need

* small kitchen sponge
* small bowl
* red and green food coloring
* latex gloves
* 4-fluid ounce (118-mL) bottle of white craft glue
* wax paper
* scissors

Fake vomit is just as good at grossing people out as fake poop. This gag will make people gag!

Step 1: Tear the sponge into little pieces. Drop the pieces into the bowl and dribble drops of red and green food coloring over them.

Step 2: Put on the latex gloves. Use your fingers to mix the colors into the pieces. Then pour the glue over them. Use your fingers to evenly coat the sponge pieces.

Step 3: Pour the mixture onto a sheet of wax paper. Let it dry for three days.

Step 4: When it's hard, peel the vomit off the wax paper. Trim any jagged edges with a scissors.

Step 5: Place the vomit wherever it will get you the biggest reaction.

Impressiveness: ★★ **Complexity:** ★★

SCARED YA!

What You Need

* ¼ cup (60 mL) water
* ¾ cup (175 mL) light corn syrup
* small bowl
* mixing spoon
* red food coloring
* chocolate syrup

Who says you have to save fake blood for Halloween? With this trick, you can get a good scare from victims any time of the year.

Step 1: Mix water and corn syrup in the bowl.

Step 2: Stir in drops of food coloring. Keep adding drops until the shade is as red as real blood.

Step 3: Stir in drops of chocolate syrup a little bit at a time. The brown color will make your fake blood look real. Don't add too much syrup or the mixture will get too runny.

Step 4: Let the mixture sit in the bowl for 10 minutes. While you wait, put on some old clothes because the mixture might stain your clothing.

Step 5: Smear the fake blood on your face, neck, or body. Then go find a victim to scare!

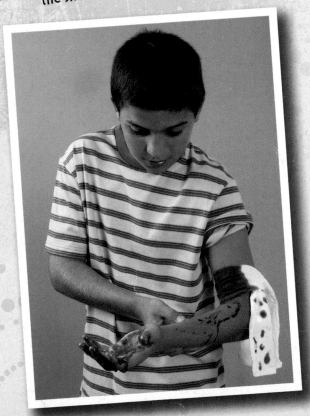

Impressiveness: ★ ★ ★   **Complexity:** ★ ★ ☆

IT'S A GUSHER!

What You Need

* large pitcher   * water   * bathroom close to a group of people

This bathroom trick is a nifty way to embarrass your parents. Consider it a "must do" at their next big party.

Step 1: When no one is around, fill the pitcher with water.

Step 2: Hide the pitcher in the bathroom.

Step 3: When a crowd is standing near the bathroom, politely announce that you need to use the bathroom.

Step 4: Close the door behind you. Then pour your hidden water into the toilet as slowly as possible.

Step 5: Flush the toilet and walk out. As you pass by the crowd, say, "Man, I sure am thirsty!"

Impressiveness: ★★☆   **Complexity:** ★☆☆

PEE YEEEWW!

What You Need

* small cup   * water   * yellow food coloring

Do your brothers and sisters get up in the middle of the night to pee? Then this practical joke is perfect! You could save it for a sleepover, but you probably won't be invited back!

Step 1: Fill the cup half full with water.

Step 2: Add drops of food coloring to the water until it looks like pee.

Step 3: Use your fingers to flick drops of the fake pee on the open toilet seat and on the floor all around the toilet.

If your victim doesn't step or sit in the fake pee, he or she will certainly see it. Be prepared for shouts of, "Eew, gross!"

Impressiveness: ★★☆   **Complexity:** ★☆☆

SECRET LETTERS

What You Need

* a fresh lemon
* knife
* small bowl
* fine-tip paintbrush
* white paper
* blow dryer

You need to get a top secret message to a friend, but how? Start squeezing. With just a lemon, your privacy is a slam dunk.

Step 1: Carefully cut a lemon into wedges with a knife. Squeeze the juice from each wedge into the bowl.

Step 2: Dip the paintbrush into the lemon juice. Wipe large drops of juice against the side of the bowl.

Step 3: Write your message on a sheet of white paper. Let the juice dry.

Step 4: Then pass the piece of paper to your friend. Tell him to heat the paper with a blow dryer. The **acid** in the lemon juice turns brown when heated. Your message will magically appear.

« **acid** a substance that tastes sour and that can burn your skin »

Impressiveness: ★★▪ **Complexity:** ★☆▪

What You Need

* ★ dollar bill
* ★ 2 small paper clips

This trick is simple, yet it's impressive for anyone who sees it for the first time. You fold a dollar bill together with loose paper clips. But when you unfold the bill, the paper clips are "magically" linked together.

2 & 3

22

Step 1: When you have an audience, grab your dollar bill and two paper clips.

Step 2: Fold the left end of the bill about a third of the way to the right edge.

Step 3: Paper clip the two layers of the bill together along its top edge. The paper clip should be centered on the folded portion.

Step 4: Fold the right end of the bill behind and toward the left edge. Push the end a little past the edge.

4 & 5

Step 5: As you did in step 3, paper clip the two new layers of the bill together along the top edge. The front of the second paper clip slips through the folded loop on the left.

Impressiveness: ★★☆   **Complexity:** ★★☆

Step 6: Show your audience the front and back of the bill. They will see one clip on one side of the bill. The second clip will be on the other side of the bill.

Step 7: Now grasp the two ends of the bill and pull it apart hard. Say, "Watch as the two paper clips magically link together!"

Step 8: After the paper clips fly off, pick them up to show the audience they are indeed joined.

DIVE-BOMBING EGG

What You Need

* hard-boiled egg
* 16-fluid ounce (473 mL) glass juice bottle
* 4 matches and a matchbook

Ever seen a boiled egg shrink and squeeze into an opening smaller than itself? Neither have your friends — until now.

Step 1: Peel the hard-boiled egg.

Step 2: Stand an empty glass juice bottle on a table.

Step 3: Set the egg upright on the mouth of the bottle. Show your friends that there is no way the egg will fit through the mouth of the bottle. Then remove the egg.

Step 4: Hold four matches together by their bottom ends. Light them all at once. Ask an adult to do this part if you don't like to use matches.

Step 5: Hold the lit matches over the mouth of the bottle for a few seconds. Give them time to burn down a little.

Impressiveness: ★★★   Complexity: ★★☆

Step 6: Drop the matches into the bottom of the bottle. Quickly balance one end of the egg on the bottle like you did in step 3.

25

TIP: MAKE SEVERAL HARD-BOILED EGGS. YOUR FRIENDS WILL WANT TO SEE THIS TRICK MORE THAN ONCE.

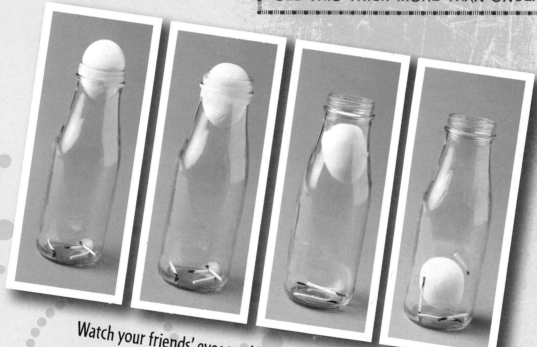

Watch your friends' eyes pop! The heat of the matches will slowly squeeze the egg and suck it into the bottle! The egg will return to its normal shape after it drops into the bottle.

JUMPING ACES

What You Need

* four aces from a deck of cards

This magic card trick is easy to master in seconds. But the audience may never figure out how you're pulling the wool over their eyes.

Step 1: Pull the four aces from a deck of cards. Set the rest of the deck aside.

Step 2: Fan the four cards toward your audience so they see the four aces.

Step 3: Put the cards back to back, so that a red ace and a black ace are in each hand.

Step 4: Hold the pairs out to your audience so that both black aces are facing them.

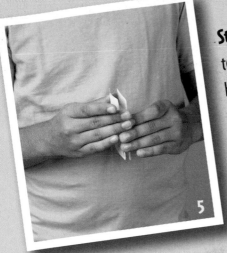

Step 5: Bring the aces close together in your hands so the black aces face each other. The red aces will face your palms.

Step 6: Wrap your fingers around the side of the cards closest to your audience. This hides that you're holding the cards in your left hand by your right middle finger and right thumb. Likewise, the right-hand cards are held by your left middle finger and left thumb.

Step 7: Bring the cards up to your lips and blow hard on them as you pull your hands down and apart. The blowing is to cover up that you're pulling the cards in your left hand down with your right fingers. This makes the red ace in your left hand face the outside.

Step 8: Show the audience that the red aces are now facing them. They'll be amazed!

Step 9: Blow on the cards again and flip the aces back to black. The secret to mastering this trick is to move your hands so quickly that the audience doesn't catch on.

Impressiveness: ★★☆   **Complexity:** ★★★

GOING UP!

What You Need
* large wall mirror   * short stool

Step 1: Ask an adult to help you lift a mirror off a wall.

This **levitation** illusion works best with the element of surprise! Ask an adult to help you set it up before you call in your friends. They won't believe their eyes!

Step 2: Lay the mirror on its side in a doorway.

Step 3: Lean about one-third of the mirror against the wall, so it stands up. Leave most of the mirror in the doorway so you can get behind it.

Step 4: Place a short stool behind the mirror.

Step 5: Stand on the stool with one leg. Dangle your other leg in front of the mirror.

Step 6: Call your friends over. Say that you have something cool to show them. To their surprise, it will look like you're floating in the air.

« **levitation** the act of rising and floating in the air »

Impressiveness: ★★☆   **Complexity:** ★☆☆

ICY DEAL

What You Need

* * ice cube
* * small glass of water
* * 6-inch (15-centimeter) piece of string
* * table salt

Step 1: Put an ice cube in a small glass of water.

Step 2: Tell your friends you are going to lift the ice cube by laying a piece of string on the ice cube. Ask if any of them would like to try it first.

This nifty trick is actually a mini science experiment. Perfect it, and you could pocket some easy cash. Bet your friends that you can pick up an ice cube with just a piece of string.

Step 3: After they fail, show them how it's done.

Step 5: Count to five, then gently lift the string. The ice cube lifts out of the water. Why? Because the salt thaws the ice cube for a second, then it refreezes. When it does, the string freezes to the cube.

Step 4: Lay the string on top of the ice cube. Then sprinkle the ice cube with table salt.

Impressiveness: ★☆☆☆   **Complexity:** ★☆★■

acid (ASS-id) — a substance that tastes sour and that can burn your skin

confess (kuhn-FESS) — to admit that you have done something wrong

embarrass (em-BA-ruhss) — to cause someone else to feel shame

levitation (lev-i-TAY-shuhn) — the act of rising and floating in the air

victim (VIK-tuhm) — a person who is tricked or hurt

vomit (VOM-it) — food and stomach acid brought up from your stomach

30

READ MORE

Klutz. *The Encyclopedia of Immaturity.* Palo Alto, Calif.: Klutz, 2007.

Mason, Tom, and Dan Danko. *Funny Magic: How to Do Tricks that Make People Laugh!* Top Secret Magic. New York: Scholastic, 2007.

Smith, Dian G. *World's Greatest Practical Jokes: Tricks to Fool Your Family, Teachers, & Friends.* New York: Sterling, 2004.

INTERNET SITES

FactHound offers a safe, fun way to find educator-approved Internet sites related to this book.

Here's what you do:

1. Visit *www.facthound.com*
2. Choose your grade level.
3. Begin your search.

This book's ID number is 9781429622752.

FactHound will fetch the best sites for you!

INDEX

32

ABOUT THE AUTHOR

Sheri Bell-Rehwoldt admits to loving a great practical joke — though she'd rather be on the giving end. Why? Because she remembers all the pranks her father pulled on her when she was growing up. She still hates grasshoppers and snakes!

Sheri is an award-winning writer and author. She has published numerous children's books, including *You Think It's Easy Being the Tooth Fairy?*